DISCARD

American Lives

Medgar Evers

Heidi Moore

Heinemann Library
Chicago, Illinois

© 2006 Heinemann Library
a division of Reed Elsevier Inc.
Chicago, Illinois

Customer Service 888-454-2279
Visit our website at www.heinemannraintree.com

Designed by Q2A Creative

Printed in China by WKT Limited

10 09 08 07 06
10 9 8 7 6 5 4 3 2 1

Library of Congress Cataloging-in-Publication Data
Moore, Heidi, 1976-
  Medgar Evers / Heidi Moore.
    p. cm. – (American lives)
  Includes bibliographical references and index.
  ISBN 1-4034-7272-6 (hc) – ISBN 1-4034-7273-4
    (pb)
  1. Evers, Medgar Wiley, 1925-1963–Juvenile
literature. 2. African American civil rights workers–
Mississippi–Jackson–Biography–Juvenile literature.
3. African Americans–Mississippi–Jackson–
Biography–Juvenile literature. 4. Mississippi–Race
relations–Juvenile literature. 5. Jackson (Miss.)–
Biography–Juvenile literature. I. Title. II. Series:
American lives (Heinemann Library (Firm))
  F349.J13M66 2006
  323'.092–dc22

                    2005010126

Acknowledgments
The author and publishers are grateful to the
following for permission to reproduce copyright
material:

AP/Wide World Photos pp. **12** (Terence Nimox), **19**,
23; Corbis pp. **5**, **13**, **18**, **22**, **24** (Flip Schulke);
Corbis/Bettmann pp. **7** (Ami Vitale), **6**, **8**, **9**, **11**, **14**,
16, **17**, **20**, **26**, **28**; Corbis/Hulton-Deutsch Collection
p. **27**; David Deardorff p. **25**; Getty Images/Hulton
Archive p. **4**; Getty Images/Time Life Pictures pp.
10, **15** (John Storey); Take Stock **21**, **29** (Matt
Herron).

Cover photograph of Medgar Evers from 1962
reproduced with permission of AP/Wide World.

Every effort has been made to contact copyright
holders of any material reproduced in this book.
Any omissions will be rectified in subsequent
printings if notice is given to the publisher.

Some words are shown in bold, **like this**. You can
find out what they mean by looking in the glossary.

Contents

A Civil Rights Leader

Medgar Evers was an important **civil rights** leader and a famous African American. He grew up in the South in a time when African Americans faced different forms of inequality. One of the forms was **segregation**, which meant that African Americans were forced to use separate public buildings and go to separate schools.

This photo of Medgar was taken in 1963.

The Life of Medgar Evers

1925	1942	1946	1948
Born on July 2 in Decatur, Mississippi	*Joined U.S. Army and served in World War II*	*Returned home to Mississippi*	*Entered college at Alcorn A&M*

But Medgar fought against this unfairness. He did well in school and worked hard to get an education. Then he became an **activist** and worked toward ending segregation. He once said, "The things I don't like I will try to change."

Thousands marched for civil rights in the 1960s.

He gave his life in the struggle for equal rights. Even though he faced difficulty, Medgar was always hopeful about the future and believed in using peaceful means to achieve his goals. His early death **inspired** a generation to join the civil rights movement and fight for equality for all Americans.

1951	1952	1954	1958	1963
Married Myrlie Beasley on December 24	*Graduated from college with business degree*	*Became field secretary for NAACP*	*Arrested for sitting on bus*	*Shot and killed on June 12*

Born in Mississippi

Medgar went to a segregated school like this one. Segregated schools often did not have enough classroom supplies.

Medgar Wiley Evers was born on July 2, 1925, in the small town of Decatur, Mississippi. His parents were James and Jessie Evers. Together, they owned a small farm. They raised pigs, cows, and chickens for food. To make some extra money, his father also worked at a sawmill.

Jessie did laundry for families in the area. Another of Medgar's chores was milking the cows.

When he was old enough, Medgar went to Decatur Consolidated School and then Newton High School. Both of these schools were **segregated**, or for African Americans only. Medgar had to walk twelve miles each way to high school, while the white students rode the bus. Medgar was not allowed to ride the bus because it was segregated, too.

In the summer, Medgar loved swimming in swimming holes, or deep spots in creeks or rivers. He also loved to go fishing.

Trouble in the South

Growing up in Mississippi in the 1930s and 1940s was difficult for African Americans because of **racism**. Sometimes white children threw things at Medgar and his brother and sisters and called them names. Many states in the South, including Mississippi, even had **Jim Crow laws**. These were laws that kept black people separate from white people in public places like schools and restaurants. These unfair laws led to widespread **segregation**.

Protestors campaigned at the White House against racism.

Medgar found work in Chicago in meat-packing plants.

Medgar learned early how **prejudice** could lead to violence. When Medgar was about eleven years old, a family friend was **lynched**, or killed, by a group of white men. Lynching was a terrible form of violence due to racism.

Despite facing racism and unfairness, Medgar worked hard and did well in school. The summer after his junior year of high school, he traveled to Chicago to work in meat-packing plants and on construction jobs. He saved money to bring back to Mississippi.

Going to War

In the war, Evers served in a segregated unit.

Medgar joined the U.S. Army in 1942. He was eighteen. During this time, the United States was fighting in World War II. Medgar served in a **segregated** unit and fought in France against German troops and then in Germany.

He left the army in 1946 when his tour of duty ended. Then he went back to live with his family in Decatur. His brother Charles also came home from fighting in World War II. After serving their country, the two young men decided to **register** to vote. At the time, this was a brave decision because **Jim Crow laws** and **discrimination** kept most African Americans from voting.

On election day, an angry **mob** of white residents blocked the polling place. This is where people go to vote. The mob would not let the Evers brothers vote. Medgar and Charles were angry. They had fought for their country, but still they did not have the same rights as other citizens.

In the Jim Crow South, African Americans were often denied the same rights as other citizens. They could rarely vote.

Back to School

In 1948 Medgar went back to school. He was twenty-three years old. He attended Alcorn Agricultural and Mechanical College (Alcorn A&M) in Lorman, Mississippi, as a business major. A popular student, he joined many campus groups and activities. He participated in debate, choir, football, and track. He also edited the campus newspaper.

Myrlie and Charles Evers attend a ceremony in honor of Medgar at Alcorn State University in 2003.

On December 24, 1951, he married a student named Myrlie Beasley. The following year, 1952, he graduated with a degree in business.

After graduation, Medgar took a job as a traveling salesperson for Magnolia Mutual Life Insurance. It was an African-American-owned company. He and Myrlie moved to Mound Bayou,

Myrlie holds their son Darrell.

Mississippi. They had three children together—two sons and one daughter.

Joining the NAACP

Medgar Evers bravely fought for equal rights.
Here he is arrested for protesting.

While traveling around the South on business, he saw the hardships that poor African-American **sharecroppers** faced. These farmers worked long hours doing hard physical labor and did not receive a fair share of the crops. Most of the crops went to the white farmers who owned the land and not to the workers. The sharecroppers were paid very little money to work the land.

Medgar thought this was unfair. As a member of the local chapter of the **National Association for the Advancement of Colored People (NAACP)** to work for equality for African Americans.

First he became a **recruiter**. He handed out voter registration forms to people as he went door to door selling insurance. He also organized **boycotts** of gas stations that would not allow African Americans to use their restrooms.

Medgar holds his son, Darrell, in 1958.

Becoming a Leader

In 1954, the Supreme Court heard the famous case **Brown versus Board of Education**. The case involved a segregated school in Topeka, Kansas. The decision was very important because it made **segregation** unconstitutional, or against the law of the land.

Medgar Evers and James Meredith speak at a press conference in 1963.

Many white people did not want schools to be **desegregated**. These African-American students needed armed guards to escort them into school.

Medgar decided to test this new law by applying to the University of Mississippi Law School. He was the first African American to apply to the all-white school. Even though segregation was illegal, the school would not admit him because of **discrimination**.

At the time, Medgar was still on the staff of the **NAACP** as a **recruiter.** The organization was proud of his strong action and decided to create a special position for him. He quit his insurance job and went to work full time for the NAACP as the Mississippi field secretary. It was the only paid NAACP position in the state.

Fighting for Justice

Protesters gather at the Mississippi State Capitol in 1962.

As the **NAACP** field secretary for the state of Mississippi, Medgar worked hard to gain **civil rights** for African Americans. He moved his family to the state capital of Jackson, Mississippi, and traveled around the state urging people to join the NAACP and collecting dues for the group.

In his first four years as field secretary, Medgar was successful at opening many more local chapters, or groups, of the NAACP. He also **investigated** violent crimes against African Americans. He reported these crimes to the newspapers to make sure such violence did not go unnoticed. He formed a council in Jackson to prevent violence against African Americans.

Medgar Evers was an **activist** who believed in hard work and peaceful action. A supporter of **integration**, he looked forward to a time when black and white residents of Mississippi could live together in peace.

Medgar worked hard as field secretary for the NAACP.

A Changing Country

During the 1950s and 1960s, the struggle for **civil rights** was heating up. Thousands of black and white people across the country were joining the fight for equality. In Mississippi, Medgar was becoming a civil rights leader. He organized **protests** to fight for equal access to schools, restaurants, and other public facilities.

Rosa Parks made her famous bus protest in 1955, three years before Medgar did the same in Mississippi.

In 1958 Medgar was arrested in Meridian, Mississippi, for sitting in a seat in the white section of a public bus. Because of **segregation** and **Jim Crow laws**, African Americans were forced to sit in one area of the bus, while white people sat in another. Even though segregation was illegal at the time, it continued in many areas of the South, including Mississippi.

Many people joined the fight for equal rights. Here **activists** in Mississippi prepare to **register** voters.

Two years later, in 1960, Medgar was sentenced to thirty days in jail and fined $100 for speaking out against an unfair court ruling against another African American. Later a Mississippi court overturned, or ruled against, that sentence.

Threats of Violence

At the time certain white people in the South did not want African Americans to have power or **civil rights.** They hated Evers because he was becoming a powerful leader in the struggle for equality.

In 1962 Medgar helped James Meredith, another African American, fight to gain a place at the University of Mississippi, the same place Medgar had tried to apply in 1954. But where Evers had failed, James

Medgar helped integrate the University of Mississippi. Many white people were angry and protested.

Meredith succeeded in getting in. This was a big step toward achieving **integration** of colleges in Mississippi. But violence followed on campus, and many people in Mississippi were even angrier with Evers for this achievement.

By 1963 Medgar and his family were receiving death threats. In May of 1963 someone threw a firebomb into his house. Soon after the incident, Medgar spoke on the radio asking people in his city to stop the **discrimination**. He said, "The **NAACP** believes that Jackson can change if it wills to do so."

James Meredith enters the University of Mississippi in 1962.

An Early Death

On June 11, 1963, President Kennedy spoke to the country about the importance of **civil rights**. The following day something happened that pushed thousands of people to recognize the problem of **discrimination** and **prejudice** facing the country.

After coming home late from a meeting, Medgar Evers was shot by a **racist** named Byron de la Beckwith outside his home. He died on June 12, 1963. He was just 37 years old.

This photo was taken at Medgar's home. You can see the bullet hole in the window.

This statue in Jackson, Mississippi was built in honor of Medgar Evers.

On the day of his funeral, thousands of African Americans came out to mourn his death in Mississippi. Across the country, millions of people—both black and white—were angry and upset. President John F. Kennedy sent Evers' wife a message in which he wrote of "the justice of the cause for which your husband gave his life."

A Hateful Crime

The murderer, Byron de la Beckwith, went to court twice in the late 1960s for killing Medgar Evers. Both times, the all-white juries did not find him guilty. He was finally found guilty at a third trial in 1994, 30 years after his crime.

Continuing the Fight

Medgar Evers was the first **civil rights activist** to be killed during the 1960s. His death brought the struggle for equality to the national spotlight.

The country was going through a period of difficult change, especially in the South. About two months after Medgar's death, Dr. Martin Luther King Jr. gave his famous "I Have a Dream" speech. It took place at the March on Washington on August 28, 1963. Thousands of black and white civil rights workers came out to **protest** against **segregation** and **discrimination**.

Medgar Evers' wife stands at his gravesite with their children.

Martin Luther King Jr. gives his "I Have a Dream" speech at the March on Washington in 1963.

Medgar's brother Charles, who tried to vote with him in Decatur in the 1950s, took over his position as field secretary for the **NAACP**. Later Charles Evers became mayor of Fayette, Mississippi.

Remembering Evers

President Lyndon Johnson signed the Civil Rights Act in 1964.

When Medgar Evers died in 1963, only 28,000 African Americans were registered to vote. By 1971, 250,000 were registered voters. Medgar was a leader in the **civil rights** movement. His actions set a path for those who followed him. His use of peaceful forms of **protest** such as **boycotts** paved the way for Dr. Martin Luther King Jr.

Medgar's life is proof that one person can make a difference. He encouraged black and white citizens to work together to end **segregation** and **discrimination**. Because of him, some businesses changed their unfair practices. Even in death, he brought attention to inequality and violence against African Americans in the South.

In 1963, the same year Medgar was killed, President John F. Kennedy asked Congress to pass a civil rights bill. In 1964, the Civil Rights Act was signed into law.

After Medgar's death, Myrlie continued the civil rights work her husband had died for. Here she stands with Ed King in 1963. At the time, he was the only white person from Mississippi who joined the civil rights movement.

Glossary

activist   person who takes action to support a cause

battalion   unit in the military

boycott   refuse to use a service or buy from a business, usually because the owners are doing something unfair

Brown versus Board of Education   1954 Supreme Court ruling that said it was illegal to have separate schools for African Americans

civil rights   fair and equal treatment for everyone

desegregation   ending the practice of keeping black and white people separate, especially in schools

discrimination   unfair treatment toward a person or group of people

inspired   influenced someone to do something positive

integration   bringing together of people in different racial groups

investigate   look into and study a crime to try to figure out what happened

Jim Crow laws   unfair laws that made segregation possible, especially in the South

lynching   violent act, often murder, by a group of people

mob   angry, often violent, group of people

National Association for the Advancement of Colored People (NAACP)   group formed in 1909 to work for equal rights and to battle social injustice toward persons of color, or African Americans

prejudice   dislike or fear of a person or group of people

protest   speak out against something unfair

racism   treating someone unfairly because of the color of that person's skin

racist   person who treats someone unfairly because of the color of that person's skin

recruiter   person who goes into the community to ask people to join a group

register   put on a list, especially a list of voters

segregation   keeping black and white people separate from each other

sharecropper   person who works on a farm in exchange for a share of the crops

World War II   war that took place between 1939 and 1945 and involved many countries

Places to Visit

Medgar Evers Home Museum
2332 Margaret Walker Alexander Drive
Jackson, Mississippi
(601) 981-2965

Bronze statue of Medgar Evers
4215 Medgar Evers Blvd.
Jackson, Mississippi
601-982-2867

Index